GASTRO-NAUTS

For Matthew.

Welcome to the world!

GASTRO-NAUTS

JAMES FOLEY

FREMANTLE PRESS

Greetings!
I'm Sally Tinker,
the world's foremost inventor
under the age of twelve.

This is my brother, Joe. He's a biological weapon with legs.
cough cough
Sorry Sal ...
... he got into your Nan's prunes again. They go straight through him!

*See 'Dungzilla'

Fear not, for we won't embiggenate anything today. (I promised Mum).
Instead, let's turn our attention to the Resizenator's super shrinkafying ability.
JOE - DO NOT EAT
Here are some things I prepared earlier: a shrinkafied coin, boot and rubber ducky!

Sal, should I call your therapist again?
Look closer.
Wow!
They're teeny-tiny!
S. TINKER INC. MICROSCOPIC OBJECT HANDHELD VIEWING WINDOW
MAGNIFICATION = X 1000
20c
<WHAT DO YOU CALL A CROCODILE WITH A MAGNIFYING GLASS? AN INVESTI-GATOR />

They're at least a thousand times smaller than normal. Amazing, yes?
But how could we put this technology to good use?
Ummm, we could shrink the world's rubbish!
We could miniaturise carbon dioxide emissions and reduce global warming!
we could belittle your evil nemesis, Dexter Maelstrom - but just, like, actually make him little!
Sorry, it was more of a rhetorical question. I've already built something.
YOINK

Allow me to introduce ...
JOE - DO NOT DRINK
... my greatest invention yet ...
... the smart Cybernetic Human Improvement aPparatus!
MICROSCOPIC OBJECT HANDHELD VIEWING WINDOW
S. TINKER INC.
MAGNIFICATION = X 1000
< WHAT DO YOU CALL A CROCODILE WITH A MAGNIFYING GLASS? />
< AN INVESTI-GATOR />
Or 'smartCHIP' for short.

So it's a microchip?
It's much more than that. It's a miniaturised supercomputer designed to A) enter the human body, B) locate the most powerful organ, and C) increase its power a hundredfold!
Hmm, the most powerful organ is the brain, so --

GASP! This doohickey attaches to your brain and makes you super smart?
Correct. And I'm going to test it on myself.

But ... aren't you smart enough already?
Granted, I am a genius, but one can never have too much of a good thing, right?
So, uh, how do you 'plug it in'?
Oh no, are you gonna ask me to do brain surgery? I told you, never again!
Relax. The installation process is simple: you drink from this test tube and the little robotic helpers do the rest.

S. TINKER INC. MICROSCOPIC OBJECT HANDHELD VIEWING WINDOW
MAGNIFICATION = X 1000
<SENTIENT ROBOTS AGAIN, HUH? THIS SHOULD END WELL />
MAGNIFICATION = X 10,000
See? Every one of those little dots is an artificially intelligent smartbot.
They install, maintain and protect the smartCHIP.

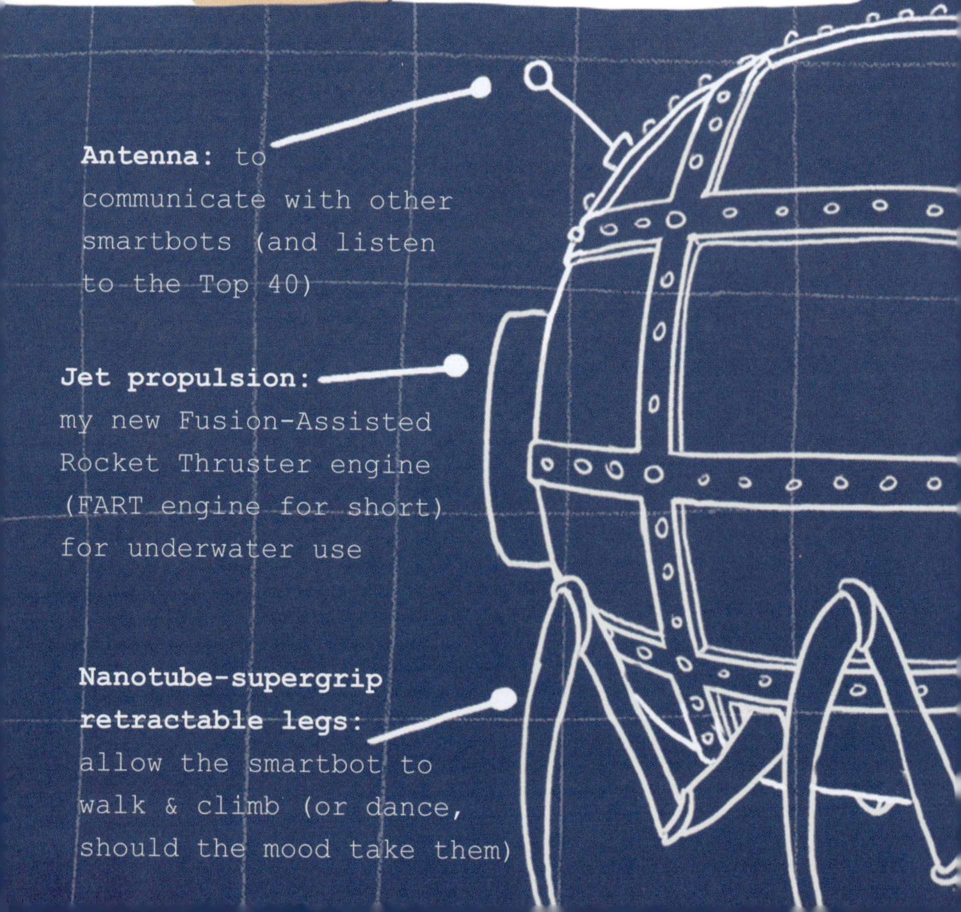
Antenna: to communicate with other smartbots (and listen to the Top 40)
Jet propulsion: my new Fusion-Assisted Rocket Thruster engine (FART engine for short) for underwater use
Nanotube-supergrip retractable legs: allow the smartbot to walk & climb (or dance, should the mood take them)

The SMARTBOT

[smartCHIP maintenance & security]

An S.TINKER INC. invention

Strong, light watertight shell: corrosion-resistant syntactic foam epoxy resin (that's a real thing I found on Wikipedia)

Evolving artificial intelligence: able to learn and modify their behaviour, so they get smarter with time (sounds totally safe)

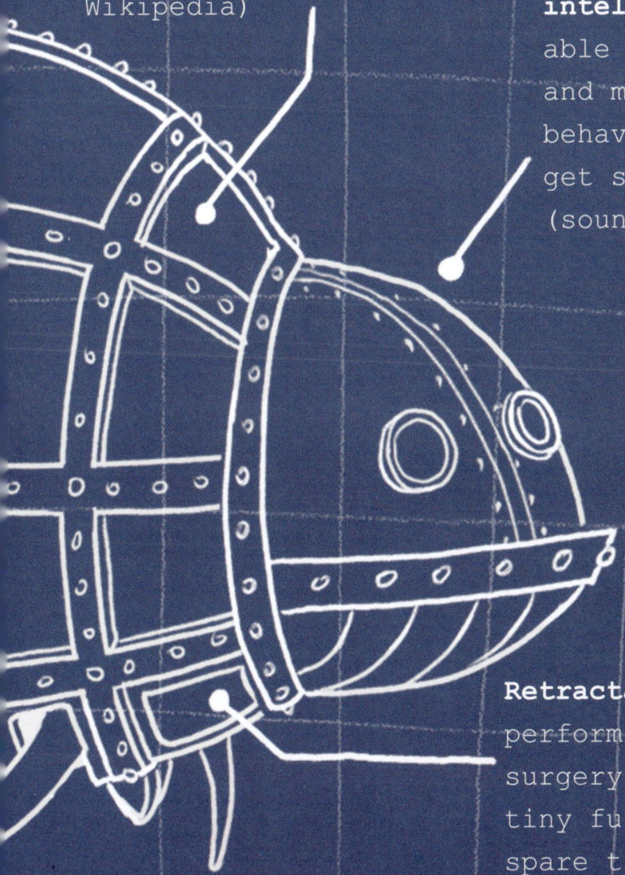

Retractable tools: for performing microscopic surgery (and building tiny furniture in their spare time)

Whoa. So how do they protect the smartCHIP?
Observe: a pencil.
If I threaten the safety of the smartCHIP like so ...
JOE - I
The smartbots will neutralise the threat.
JOE - I

And you want to put those things inside you?!
Relax! It's perfectly safe. When have any of my inventions ever gone wrong?*
*See every single other S.Tinker Inc. book
Besides, it's worth the risk. The smartCHIP will make me the smartest human who's ever lived.
I'll unlock the secrets of the universe!
I'll finally beat Nan at backgammon!

I dunno Sal.
I've got a bad feeling about this ...
JOE - DO NOT DRINK
TONK
Ow. What the--
EEEEK!!

Ah, here's the last of the smartbots, fresh off the production line.
But ... it's so big!
Indeed. It was easier to build them giant-sized and shrink them down.

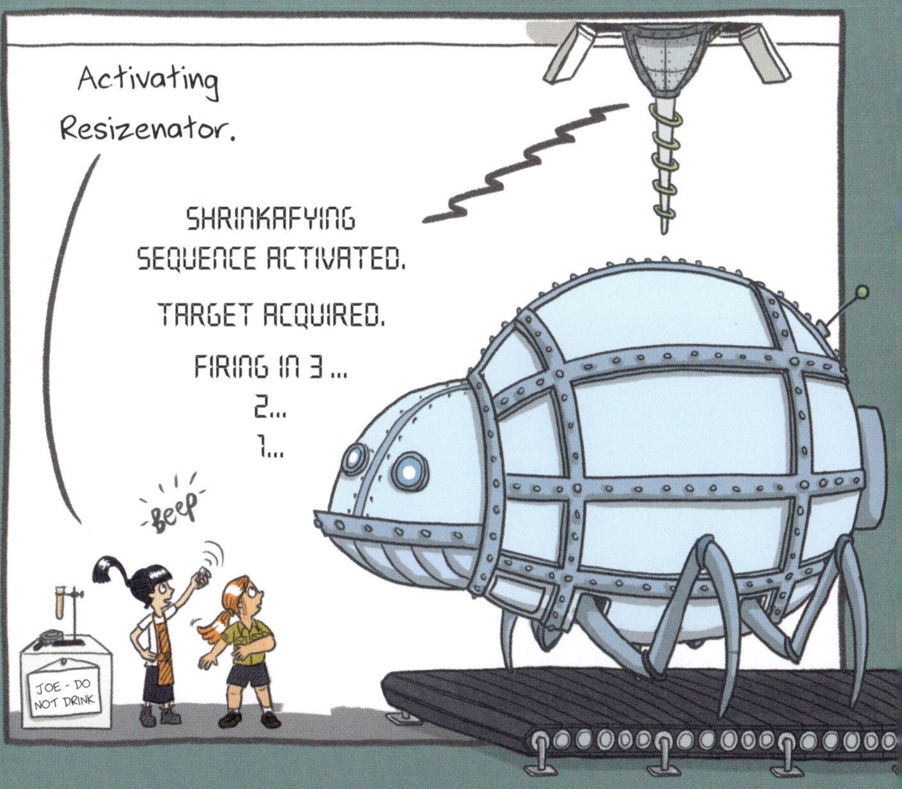
Activating Resizenator.
Beep
SHRINKAFYING SEQUENCE ACTIVATED.
TARGET ACQUIRED.
FIRING IN 3 ...
2...
1...
JOE - DO NOT DRINK

ZAP
JOE - DO NOT DRINK

SHOOM
SHOOM
SHOOM
SHOOM
JOE - DO NOT DRINK

*iGOR = 'I Grab Objects Robotically'

VZZZZZHHH
WHIRRR
iGOR
iGOR
JOE - DO NOT DRINK
WHOOOSHHH
plink
Thank you, iGOR.
You can go.
JOE - DO NOT DRINK
iGOR

We're finally ready. Watch in wonder as I, Sally Tinker, become the smartest human ever! Bottoms up ...
Wait, Sal! Are you sure you can handle being THAT smart?
Of course! I mean, I can definitely think of worse candidates.
Can you imagine if Joe became super smart? He's enough trouble as it is; with the smartCHIP he'd be a supervillain!
No, it's much safer if I test this on myself.

*Sub = Sally's Underwater Boat

So when do we set off on our oceanic adventure?
Oh Charli, you're funny. No, I thought we could use it to clean the fish tank.
What? Why don't you just use a scrubbing brush? I could clean it for you now in ten minutes, tops.
But that wouldn't be as much fun, would it! C'mon, I'll show you how it works.
Okay.
(Anything to distract you from drinking those smartbots ...)

Are you sure we'll shrink properly, Sal?
The Sub definitely will.
ENGINE ROOM
But we'll be fine ... right?
There is a small chance that the Sub will shrink while we stay the same size.

Why does it sound like there's a 'but' coming?
Well ... technically this will be the first time I shrink the Sub with human occupants.
Sub sweet Sub
The good news is, we'd be squished so quickly we wouldn't feel a thing.
EEP.

All systems ready.
Shrinkafication in 3 ... 2 ... 1 ...
ZAP

SHOOM
SHOOM
SHOOM
SHOOM
iGOR
Did it work?
See for yourself.
Whoa ...

Now to have iGOR place us in the fish tank ...
< SCANNING ... ID MATCH= SMARTBOT />
Wow, Sal ...
... iGOR got here quick.

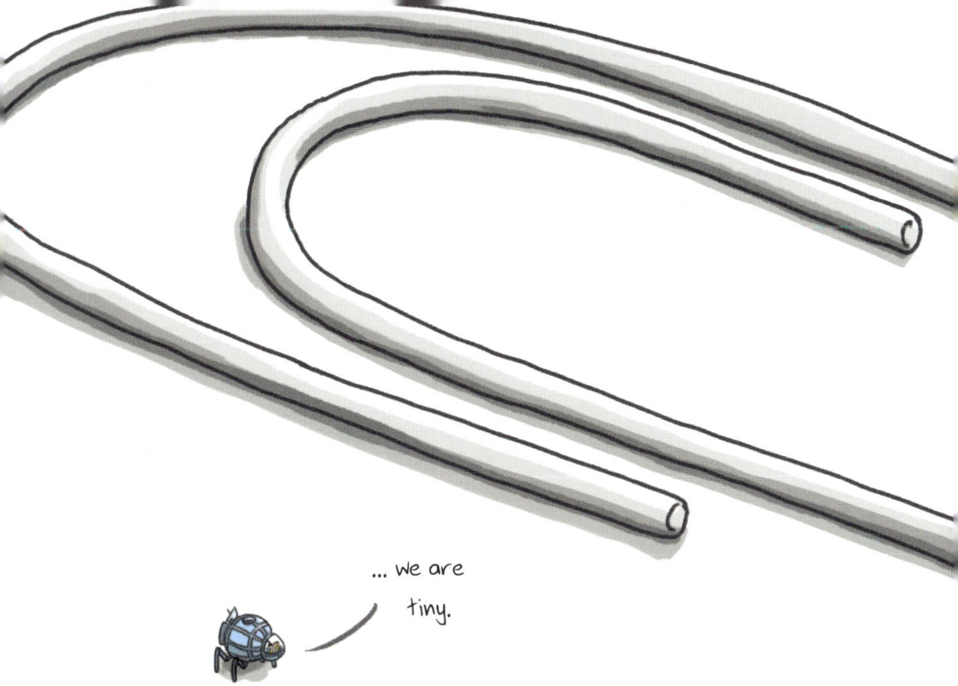
... we are
tiny.

Actually Charli, I hadn't called him yet.
Then what's going on??
JOE - DO NOT DRINK
iGOR

Uh oh.
Charli, seatbelts on NOW!

AAAAAA
AAAAAAAAAAAAAAAAAAAAAA

plink
KA-
SPLASH

Sal, this is definitely not the fish tank!
It appears iGOR thought the Sub was a smartbot, so he put us with the others. (I must update his visual recognition database ...)
Are they gonna do to us what they did to that pencil??
No, they'll think we're a smartbot too. Don't worry, everything is going to be fine.

JOE - DO NOT DRINK

Oh crud.

Joe's gonna drink us, Sal!
But I wrote a sign specifically telling him not to.
He's a baby, he can't read!!

That's no excuse. When I was his age I'd already read the entire encyclopedia. Twice!
Can we talk about something else, please? Like, for example, how we're ABOUT TO DIE??

AAAA

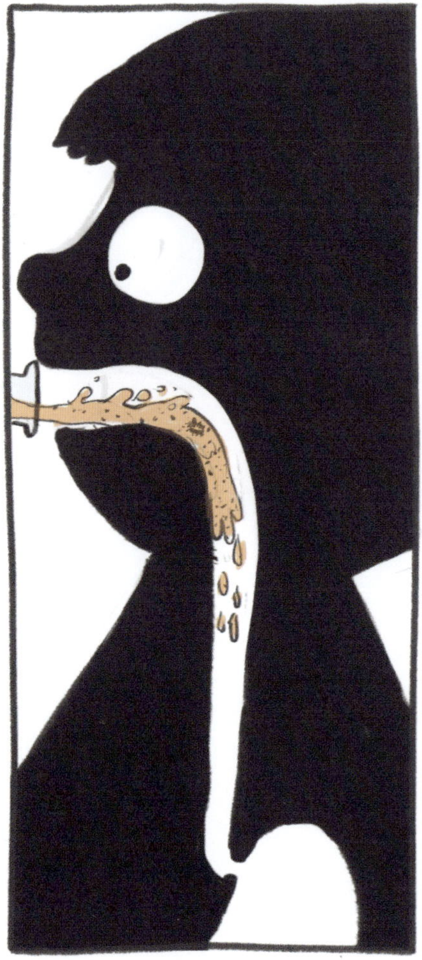

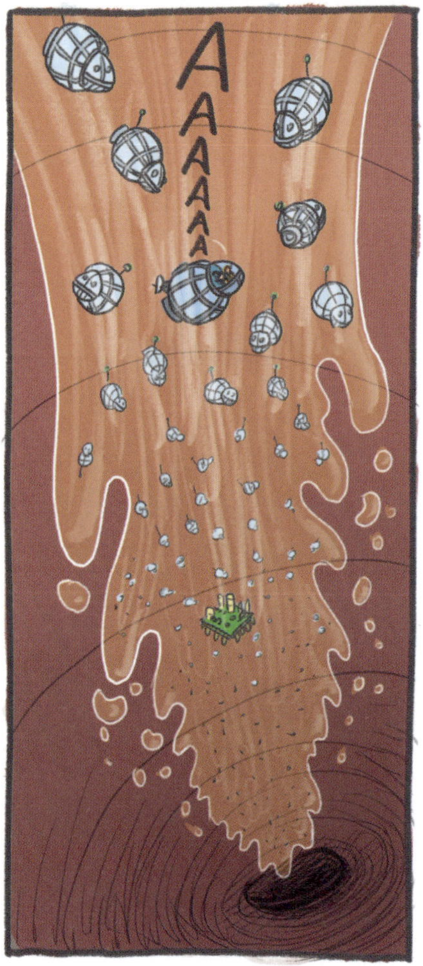
AAAAAAAA

Sal,
are you okay?
You don't look
so good.

AAAAAAAAAAA
AAAAAAAAAAAA
SPLOOSH

Here, have a sick bag.
S'just a little motion sickness, I'll be fine --
hmphgl
BLERGH
... unless you count a strawberry and some shrunken things?

BLOOP
Phew, that's better. Where are we?
In your brother's stomach.
Lucky he hasn't had any big meals lately ...
20c

Hmphgl I think I'm going to be sick again.
It could be worse: we could be in Joe's large intestine. That's where food gets fermented into farts.
And hey, at least the smartbots are gone.
Oh crud, the smartbots!! They'll be installing the smartCHIP in Joe's brain by now.
He'll be the smartest human who's ever lived.
He'll unlock the secrets of the universe.
He'll beat Nan at backgammon!!

Why don't we head for the nearest 'exit', make ourselves big again, then turn off the smartCHIP with the remote control?
Because there isn't a remote control.
Only when people are watching.
Sal! You always do this!
I couldn't let any of my many enemies tamper with the smartCHIP once it was installed in my brain ...
... so I made it super secure. It can't be shut down remotely, or hacked via wifi, or fried with an electromagnetic pulse.

The only way to shut down the smartCHIP is manually ...
... via a control panel on the smartCHIP itself ...
... which is guarded by smartbots.

It's an ingenious security set-up, if I do say so myself.
So you're saying the only way to stop your brother being super smart is to pilot the Sub all the way through his body to his brain, while avoiding an army of killer robots?
Correct! What could possibly go wrong?
Could you please plot a course from here to the brain?
I have to call Nan.

Back at S.Tinker Inc. HQ ...
Hello, rascal. Destroying your sister's experiments as usual, I see? Where's she got to, anyway?
JOE - DO NOT DRINK
BRIIINNG BRIIINNG
BRIIINNG BRIIINNG
SAL
This is her now.
Sal, where are you? You said you'd watch Joe.
We're not far. In fact, you could say we're keeping a close eye on him.

Well I'm glad you called; someone's been at my prunes. You wouldn't know what happened, would you?
Can we talk about that later? We've got a situation. Remember the smartCHIP I was working on?
The thing with the creepy little robot critters? You didn't swallow them, did you?
No, I didn't swallow them ...
Then what's the problem?
BURP

Ah.
Joe swallowed them.
Indeed.
And he swallowed something else too ...
Let me guess.
You're in the Sub, inside Joe.
Correct, but ...
I thought you'd be at least a little surprised.
You've gotta try pretty hard to surprise me.
So what's it like in the little guy's guts?
Hi Ms Tinker,
it's Charli here.
GRUMBLE
GRUMBLE
JOE - DO NOT DRINK

We're out of Joe's stomach and into his small intestine. It's gross but amazing!
Was that corn?
We're gonna slip from here into his bloodstream, then head to his, uh, head.
Sounds lovely, dear.
While you're in there, could you keep an eye out for my car keys? I think Joe might have swallowed them.
Will do, Ms Tinker.

Nan, we'll take care of the smartCHIP and smartbots. Can you keep an eye on Joe?
He'll be super smart any minute now, and he's likely to get into mischief.
Oh, and there could be side effects.
FRRT
Nan?
Nan, do you read?
Sorry Sal, a bit of distraction at this end. Well, at Joe's end. You were saying?

I said there could be side effects.
FRRRRRRRRRT
Nan, are you there?
POOT
POOT
POOT
Is something wrong??
clap clap
clap clap
clap clap
THUD

Uh, it's --
FRRRRRRRR
RRRRRRRT
SMASH

CLATTER
THUD
Nan?
Nan?!
I'm gonna hafta call you back.

She hung up!
I hope everything's okay.
Unlikely. But Nan will have to cope until we can shut down the smartCHIP.
So Charli, which way now?
We follow the red blood cells to the heart and lungs, then take the first left to Joe's brain.

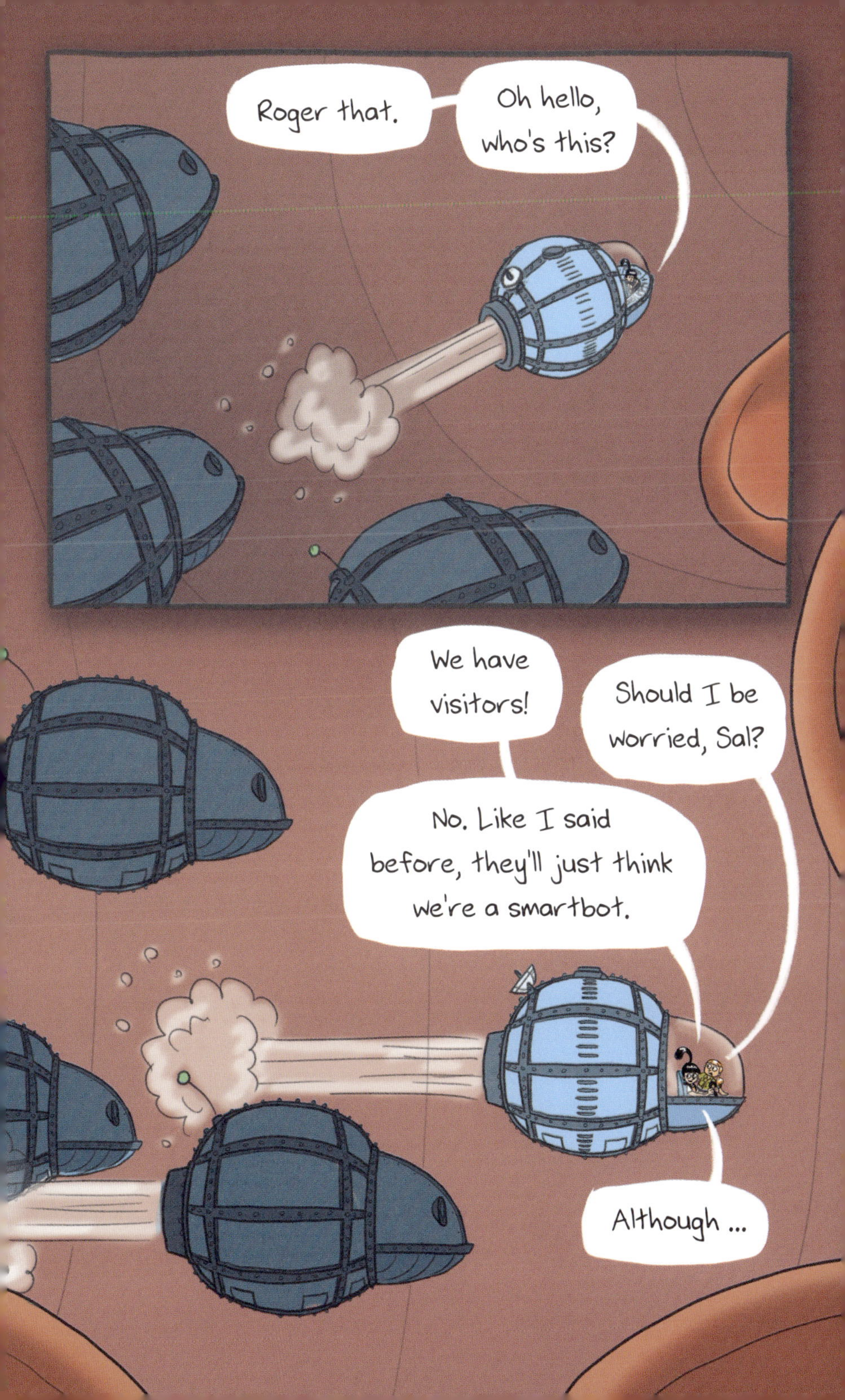

Roger that.
Oh hello, who's this?
We have visitors!
Should I be worried, Sal?
No. Like I said before, they'll just think we're a smartbot.
Although ...

... I programmed them to stay close to the smartCHIP, and they're out on patrol in the bloodstream. It's odd. Perhaps they're smarter than I anticipated.
Not too smart, I hope.
< SCANNING ... />
< SCANNING ... />
TRUE FACT #42: DID YOU KNOW THAT IF YOU TOOK ALL THE VEINS FROM YOUR BODY AND LAID THEM END TO END, YOU'D BE DEAD?
< ID MATCH = SMARTBOT. 85% MATCH ONLY />
< CLOSER OBSERVATION REQUIRED />

< SCANNING ... />
< ANOMALIES DETECTED />
< 1. PAINT: LIGHT BLUE = NON-STANDARD />
< 2. SMARTBOT SHELL: MULTIPLE UNAUTHORISED MODIFICATIONS />
< 3. TINY HUMAN PILOTS: NOW THAT I THINK ABOUT IT, KIND OF A GIVEAWAY />
TRUE FACT #73: BLOOD IS THICKER THAN WATER, BUT MAPLE SYRUP IS THICKER THAN BLOOD, SO TECHNICALLY PANCAKES ARE MORE IMPORTANT THAN FAMILY.
< ID MATCH = ~~SMARTBOT~~ ID MATCH = INTRUDER />
< ALERT ALL SMARTBOTS: INTRUDER DETECTED />
< PROTECT SMARTCHIP! DESTROY INTRUDER! />

WHIRRR...
WHIRRR...
WHIRRR...
Um, Sal? They're looking at us weird ...
WOOOOOSH!

KA-CHUNK!
KA-CHUNK!
KA-CHUNK!
Hold on!
CRUNCH

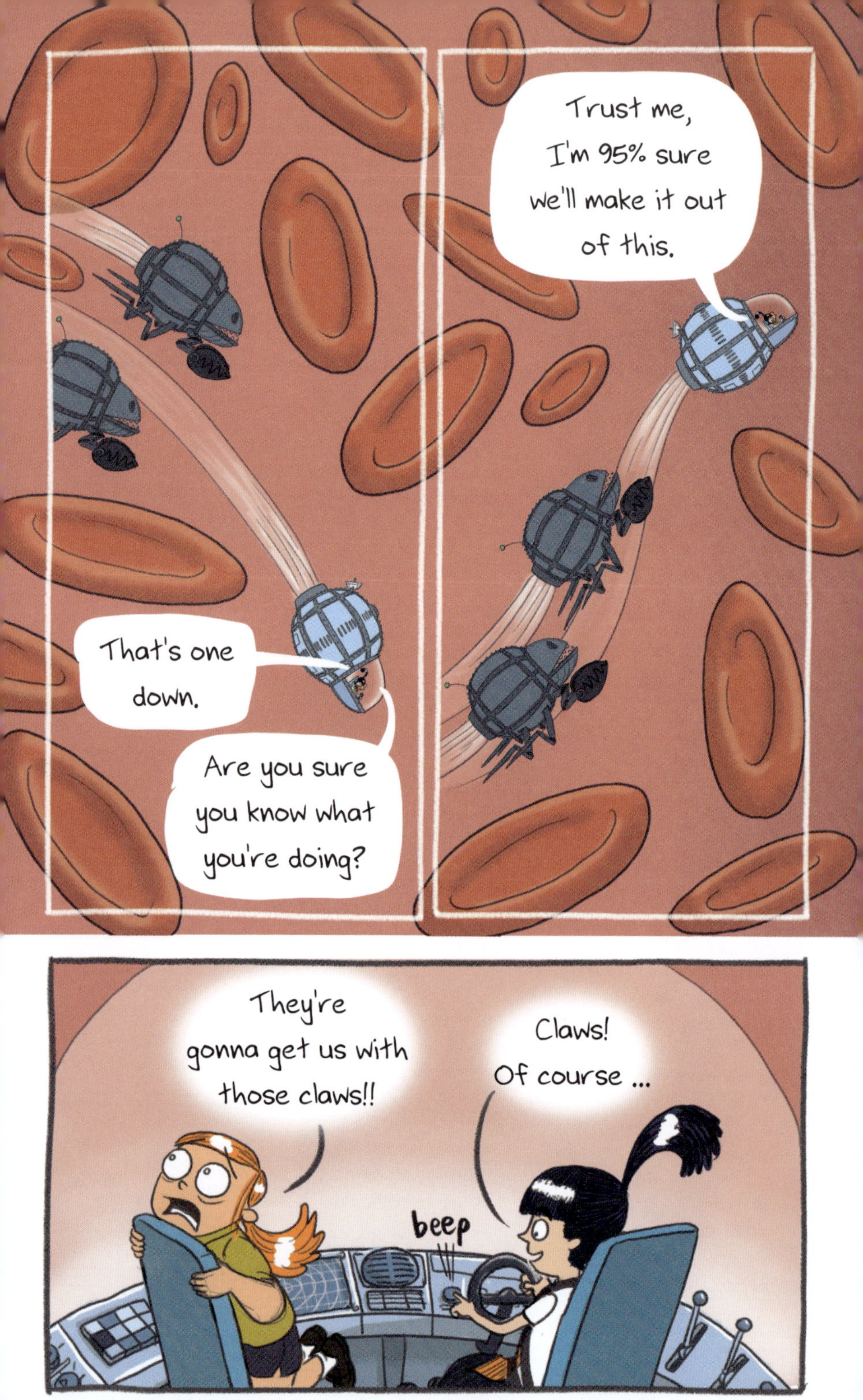
That's one down.
Are you sure you know what you're doing?
Trust me, I'm 95% sure we'll make it out of this.
They're gonna get us with those claws!!
Claws! Of course ...
beep

Actually, 59%.
Make that 5.9%.
WHIRRR...
KA-CHUNK

SNAP
SNAP
CRASH

Sal, you saved us!
For now. Look at the radar: we're surrounded.
< ALERT: SMARTBOTS APPROACHING />
TWO BLOOD CELLS MET AND FELL IN LOVE, BUT ALAS ... IT WAS ALL IN VEIN.
1 2 4 5 6 7 8 9 * 0 #
Whadda we do? We're sitting ducks!!
I may have an idea ...

< ??? />
Tesla's moustache! It worked!
That was close. We'd better stay hidden the rest of the way.

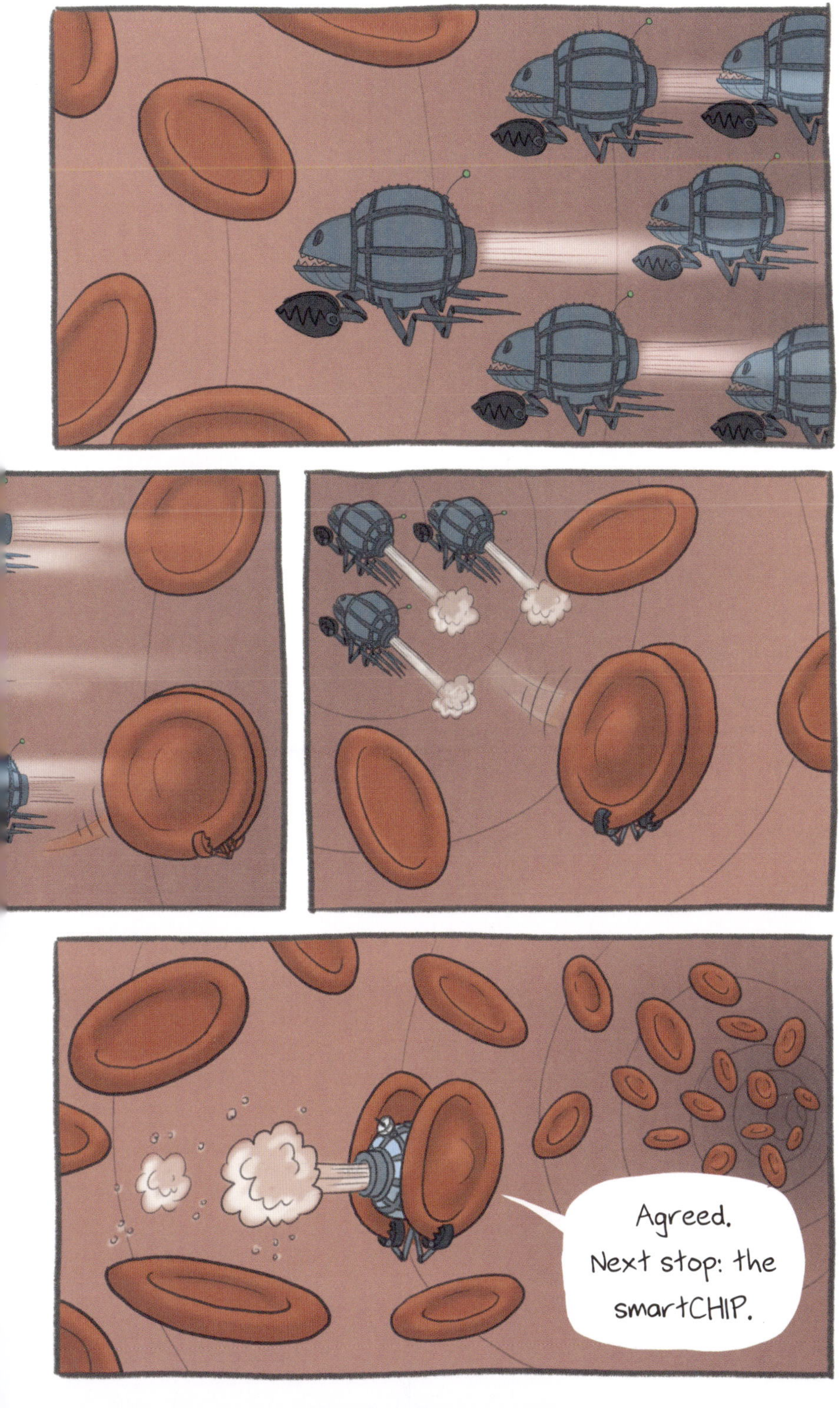
Agreed. Next stop: the smartCHIP.

Meanwhile, on the streets of Littleton ...
Look. Up in the sky!
It's a bird.
It's a plane.
It's ...
POOT
POOT
POOT
... a flatulent baby.
THUD

Miaoww!
FRRRT
Miaowwww!
It's okay Mojo.
I'll get help!
POOT
POOT
POOT

FRRRT
YOINK
Mojo!
POOT
Thanks, Super Baby!
FRRRT

BEEP
BEEP
VRRRRRMM
VRRRRRM
POOT
POOT
POOT

FRRRRRRRRRT
Thief!
ST
BUTCHER
BAKER
CAND
Stop!
Thief!

POOT
POOT
POOT
Huh?
POW
FRRRRRRT

Super Baby, you're my hero!
Clap clap clap
Clap clap clap
clap clap clap
Clap clap clap
RUMBLE
clap clap clap...
GRUMBLE
SQUEEEAK

FRRRRRRT

MY NOSTRILS!
GET BACK!
COVER YOUR NOSES!
RUMBLE

MASKS
2112
GAS MASKS -R- US
POOT
PWARP
FRRRT
BIP
FWEET

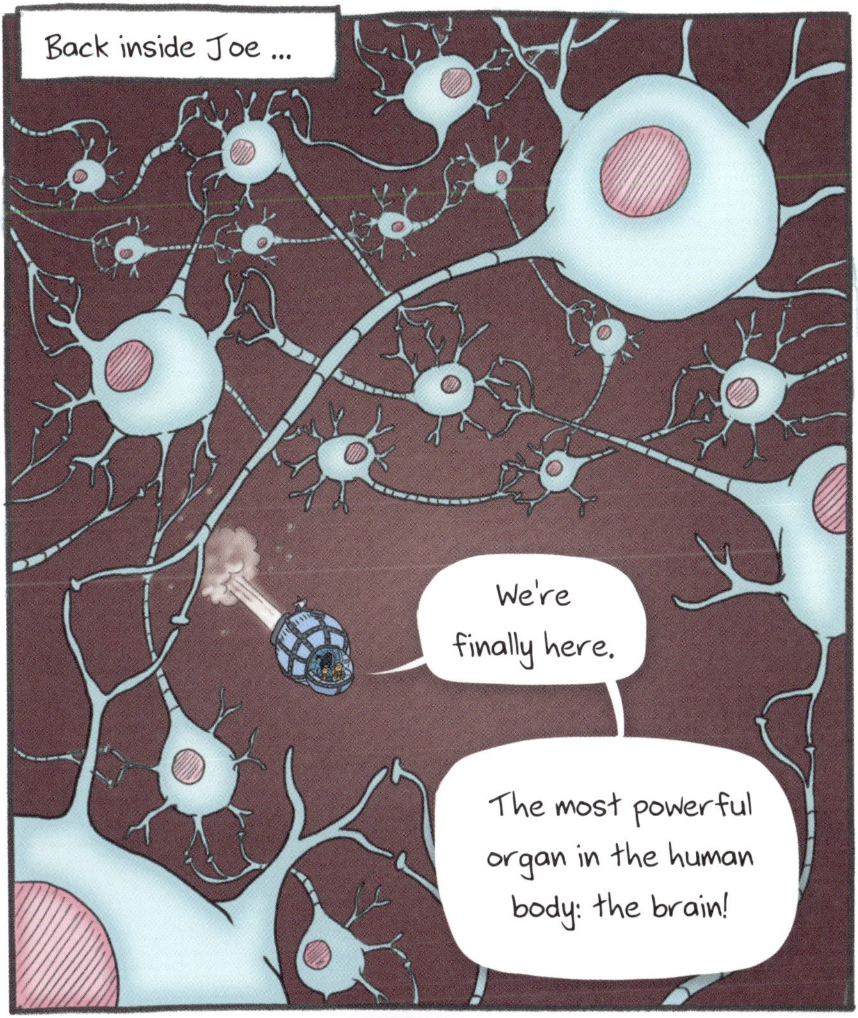
Back inside Joe ...
We're finally here.
The most powerful organ in the human body: the brain!

I expected more smartbots, though. There's none on the radar.
Radar won't work here, not with the brain's electromagnetic field.

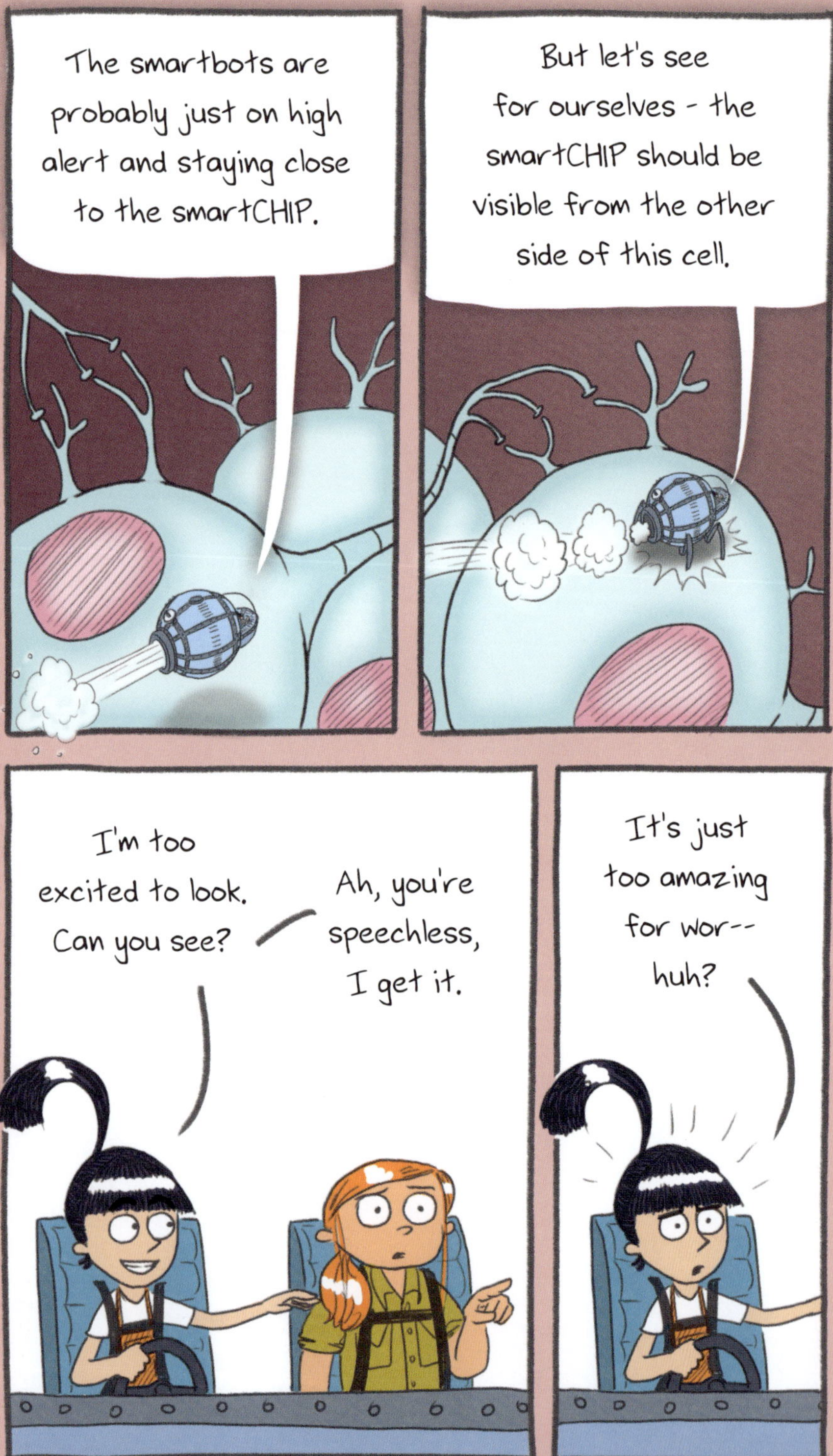
The smartbots are probably just on high alert and staying close to the smartCHIP.
But let's see for ourselves - the smartCHIP should be visible from the other side of this cell.
I'm too excited to look. Can you see?
Ah, you're speechless, I get it.
It's just too amazing for wor-- huh?

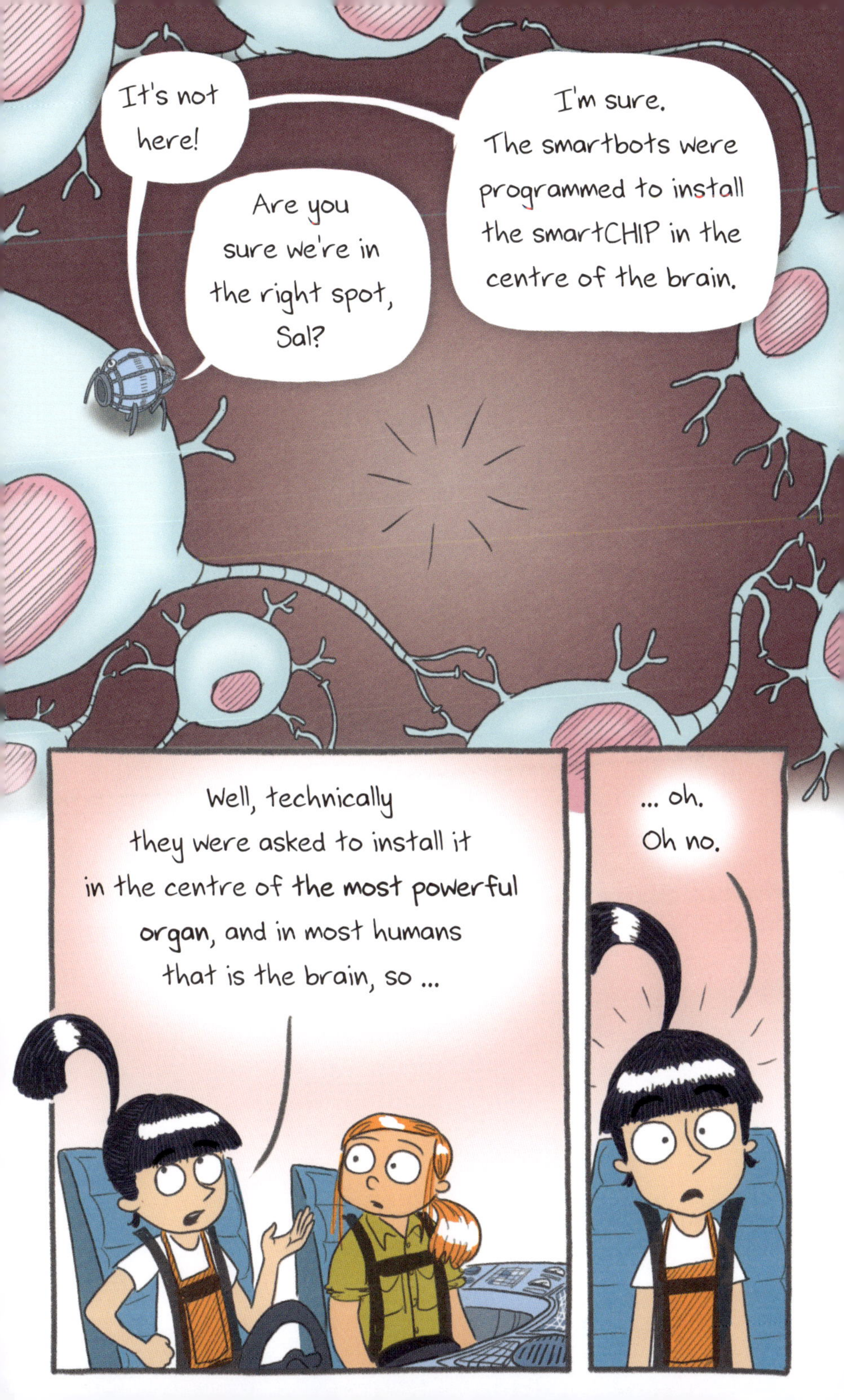

It's not here!
Are you sure we're in the right spot, Sal?
I'm sure. The smartbots were programmed to install the smartCHIP in the centre of the brain.
Well, technically they were asked to install it in the centre of the most powerful organ, and in most humans that is the brain, so ...
... oh. Oh no.

WOOOOOOSH
What is it, Sal? Where are we going?
BRIIINNG BRIIINNG
Somewhere I never wanted to go.
BRIIINNG BRIIINNG
Sal.
Joe's bottom burps are out of control.
Crud. How bad is it?

They had to evacuate the whole town; it's just too stinky.
Are you sure he swallowed a smartCHIP and not a fartCHIP?
It's as I suspected, then.
FRAPP
BRUMP
PHTHLPB
QUARANTINE
NTINE
QU
When the smartbots explored Joe's body, they found an organ more powerful than his brain.
One with more energy. More raw, untapped power. One with a large deposit of natural gas.
Oh, Sal.
You don't mean ...

Alimentary, my dear Charli ... the smartCHIP is in Joe's large intestine.
Right in the fart of darkness. The horror, the horror ...
But Sal, how is that possible?
I'm not entirely sure. But somehow, the smartbots have connected the smartCHIP to Joe's gut, increasing its power a hundredfold.
He's now the fartiest human who's ever lived.

You've gotta turn that smartCHiP off, Sal.
Plants are wilting. Birds are falling from the sky. If this goes on much longer, it's gonna be Fartageddon.
Don't worry, Nan. We'll get to the bottom of this.
Righto. Godspeed, Gastronauts.

So that's why we couldn't find any smartbots in Joe's brain - they're all in his bum with the smartCHIP!
How are we gonna get past them?
I've got a plan ... but we're not going to like it.

At the entrance of Joe's large intestine ...
< SCANNING ... />
< SCANNING ... />
< SCANNING ... />

< SCANNING ... />
< OBJECT APPROACHING ... ID MATCH = INTRUDER />

< INTRUDER DETECTED! />
< DESTROY INTRUDER! />

CRASH! BASH! SMASH!
Sploosh
They went for it. Your plan worked!
Shame that plan involved piloting through this puddle of poop.
Finally. We're here!

The smartCHIP.

It's a bit different to your original design. Looks like the smartbots did some renovations.
Astonishing! They've adapted it to suit Joe's intestine.
It appears these pipes suck up the muck ...
SLURP!
... and the vent at the top releases supercharged fart gas.
FRRRT
Ingenious. It's a work of art.
You could even say it's a work of fart.
PERI-SCOPE CAM

Indeed.
Now, the smartbots are on the lookout for the Sub, so let's keep it hidden down here.
BLOOP
SLURP

The **manual shutdown control panel** is on the platform above. I'll go up alone.
But how will you get there? I don't see a ladder.
There's only one way up ...

SLURP SLURP SLURP
... through the pipe.
I'd better suit up before I change my mind.
sub
But ... you can't go swimming in that!
It's basically liquid poop!

Believe me, if there was another way I'd take it.
But this is the only way, and the town is depending on us.
This suit will protect me from ...
... the biohazards in my brother's gizzards.

So what should I do?
Stay here, call Nan and pass on these instructions. If I can't shut down the smartCHIP, you tell Nan to initiate Plan P.
Don't you mean 'Plan B'?
No, it's definitely a 'P'.
PLAN P
Okay, got it. Good luck!
Gee, I hope Sal knows how to swim ...
BRIIING
BRIIING

Girls, talk to me.
Hi Ms. Tinker, Charli here.
Sally asked if you could grab something from the supermarket.
This isn't the time for a spot of shopping!
PLAN P
She said you'd say that. Then she told me to tell you it was vital to the plan, and you're her favourite grandma.
But I'm her only grandma! Okay, fine. What does she need?
PLAN P
Meanwhile:
Okay. Relax, Sal.

This is going to be fine. Totally not gross at all.
Oh who am I kidding, this is gonna be the grossest thing ever. ICK!
Ok, on 3.
1 ...
2 ...
... whoa
WHOA--
SLIP
AAAAAAAAAAAAA
PLOP

SLURP
GROSS GROSS GROSS GROSS
SLURP
SLURP
GROSS
GROSS
GROSS
GROSS
SLURP
GROOOOOOSS ...

CREEPY AND GROSS
SLURP
SUPER GROSS
SLURP
GROOOOOOOSSSSSS

creeak...
SPLOSH
Gross.

< SCANNING ... />
Okay Sally, focus. Get past the smartbots, find the control panel.
Oh well. Makes it easier for me!

There it is!
But where are the guards?
Now to shut down the smart--
< HELLO INTRUDER />
Oh crud.
< CAUGHT YOU, LOL :P :P :P />

WOOP WOOP WOOP
WOOP
WOOP
WOOP
<IT'S A TRAP />
GASP
WOOP WOOP WOOP
WOOP WOOP WOOP
Clever girl ...

Hello.
I, uh, like what you've done with the place ...
<IT'S A TRAP />
Charli, come in! Tell Nan to initiate Plan P then get yourself out of here --
EEEEEEEEEP!
YOINK

< INTRUDER DETECTED! />
EEEEEEEEEEEEEP!
< DESTROY INTRUDER! />

Ch-Charli?
I gotcha, Sal. Hold on.

Uh oh.
CLUNK
< DESTROY INTRUDER! />
Whadda we do now, Sal?
Not yet.
Have you told Nan the plan?
Then I'll do that. You get us to higher ground.

How am I supposed to do that?
Just aim for the wall and let the Sub do the rest.
I hope this works ...
< DESTROY INTRUDER! />
EEEEEP!
Whoa!

Look, Sal! I'm driving you up the wall!
BRIIING
BRIIING
Not for the first time.

BRIIING
BRIIING
Sal? What's all this about a 'Plan P'?
Sorry Nan, no time to explain. Have you got the prunes?
Yes, just like you asked.
Great. Joe needs to eat all of them right now.
LAX-O-BRAND
PRUNES

Uh, Sal, just confirming ... it sounded like you want Joe to eat all the prunes.
That's affirmative.
Are you sure?
Yes I'm sure. The whole jar, NOW. It's an emergency!

Okay ... but you have to deal with the aftermath.
We won't be alive for that if you don't hurry!
Alright, hold your horses...
LAX-
Here, kiddo ...
TINE
LAX-O-BRAND
PRUNES
... have at 'em.
LAX-O-BRAND
PRUNES
clap
clap
clap
clap
clap
clap
LAX-O-BRAND
PRUNES

LAX-O-BRAND
PRUNES
SPLAT
SPLOT
SLURP
SPLOTCH
BURP
Sal, are you sure that was a good idea? Prunes go straight through Joe.
I know, Charli. I'm counting on it.

FRRRT
But they'll go straight through his stomach ...
Mm-hmm ...
... then straight through his small intestine ...
... yeees ...
... then straight to his large intestine ...
... indeed ...
... which is where we are!
... correct.
Brace yourself, Charli ...
... the prunes are coming.

RUMBLE
RUMBLE

Sal, it's a tsunami!
A poo-nami! A prune-ami!
EEEEP!

KA-
Hold on!
< SCREEEE! />

SPLODGE
< SCREEEE! />
< SCREEEE! />

< SCREEEEEEEEEE! />
Hahaha! Sal!
Are you okay, Charli?
Yep, I just figured out what the 'P' in 'Plan P' stood for!
FRRT
FRRT

Hahahaaahaaaa actually I think I'm in shock.
Agreed. Though it's understandable when one nearly suffers death by prune and poop.
I think Joe's in for a shock, too.
BLIB
BLUB
BLoop
BLART
SO. Now that the smartbots are all downstream, we can finally use the control panel to shut down the smartCHIP!
Uh, Sal ...

... don't count your chickens.
Some smartbots stayed behind and the'y re headed this way!

Now we're trapped. Plus the smartCHIP is making more gas! Whaddawedo??
Quit pressuring me, I'm thinking --
That's it: pressure!
Turn us around and head for the vent.
What? Why??
Trust me!
Okay, we're at the vent ... now what??
Now, you somersault the Sub into the vent.

I can't do that!
You have to, Charli, it's the only way to escape AND shut down the smartCHIP.
Once we plug the vent, the fart gas will have nowhere to go. The pressure will build and build, until finally ...
... the smartCHIP will explode AND fire us out of Joe's bottom like a bullet from a gun.
But won't we get stuck in Joe's nappy?
Possibly. But if we're going fast enough, we'll go straight through the nappy and its contents.
Literally.
So if we stay here we meet a sticky end. If we go, we could also meet a sticky end.
Okay. It was nice knowing you, Sal ...

BOING
EEEP!
FOOMF
I did it!
Great job. Now give it a few seconds ...
PFFFT
... almost there ...
TWANG!
TWANG!
PFFFT
PFFFT

POW
AAAA
KA-BOOM!
AAAAAAAAAAAAA

AAAAAAAAAAAAAAAAAA
AAAA

QUARANTINE
QUARANTINE
QUARANTINE
GRUMBLE GRONK GRRRR
AAAAAAAAAAAAAAAAAAAAAAAAAAAAAAA
BLERGH!

Take cover, he's gonna blow!
QUARANT
hmphgl

FRRRRT

AAAAAAAAAAAA AA
P
QUARANTINE

AAAAAAAAAAAAA
QUARANTINE
P

FRRRRRRRRRRRRRRT

POOT
POOT
POOT
PFFFFFFT...
Meanwhile, on the ground ...

I gotcha, Joe!

Oh who am I kidding.
Where's Sal when you need her?
zap!
Nan!
We're back!
Where's Joe?
He'll be here any second ...
SHOOM!

...you have to do something!
Joe!
NO!!

Charli what do we do what do we do what do we do he's gonna go splat and this is all my fault and there's no time--
It's okay Sal, look!

Gotcha.
HOORAY!

Well, I must say Main Street is a bit of a mess ...
... but at least Joe is safe ...
My bad. I'll fix it.
... and thank goodness you finally passed through Joe. I wondered if I'd ever see you again!
Aw shucks, Nan.
Not you girls, I knew you'd be alright. Look!
SQUELCH
SQUILCH
Aha!
There you are.

The ^STICKY^ End

Wait!
Turn the page ...

Keep reading!
There's another brilliant
bonus story ...

GET KRAKEN

Hello! Charli Stevenson here, your friendly neighbourhood biologist.
My friends and I are on a mission to find the incredible Kraken!
Legends say it's a mega, massive sea monster ...
... we're gonna prove this majestic creature exists.

Here's the pilot: my BFF, Sally Tinker, the world's best inventor under twelve.
Greetings! And welcome to the SUB ...

... not a bad invention, if I say so myself.
The S.U.B., aka 'Sally's Underwater Boat'
17.75°N, 142.50°E
PACIFIC OCEAN
communications dish
hatch
periscope
ladder
cabin
mechanical arm compartments

Rav Mitra is on camera duties. Thanks for coming, buddy!
I don't like confined spaces. Or getting wet. Or fish. I'm fishophobic! Why did I let you talk me into this?

And this little guy is Sally's baby brother, Joe.
He was supposed to stay home with Nan, but he stowed away.
How he squeezed into the glove box, I'll never know.

We've come to the Mariana Trench, the deepest point in the world's oceans.
A few days ago, a local fishing crew reported huge tentacles towering over their ship.
They didn't get any proof ... but we will.

We're gonna find the Kraken in the pursuit of science!
SHIP REX
Well guess what, wimps? I'm gonna find it first ...
... in the pursuit of fame.
And MONEY!
Ohmigosh—that's Rex Vancouver, from MeTube!
I knew I should've packed the torpedoes.
Great. Him.

Hey, fancouvers! **Rex Vancouver** here on the hunt for the Kraken.
METUBE LIVE
1.2 BILLION LIKES
Check out my state-of-the-art luxury sub. It's got **mechanical arms**, **electro-shock nets** and **automatic emergency eject!**
Let us know what you think in the comments, fancouvers.

Ugh, 'fancouvers'. Rex thinks he's so cool.
But he IS so cool. His prank videos are legendary!
He's got over a billion followers on MeTube.
Ohmigosh, did you see him put the alligator in his mum's bath?
Ha! Remember when he hid worms in his friend's spaghetti ...
And when he put a trained lion in that school staffroom ...

Don't you see, though? He doesn't care who gets hurt by his pranks.
True. Those teachers were terrified.
Them too — but I was talking about **the animals.** They don't ask to be in his videos; they're living creatures and they deserve respect.
You're right.
But Rex seems so cool ...
He's not. If he finds the Kraken before us, who knows what he'll do with it.

So this time next week ...
expect the worldwide release of Rex's **Kraken Kalamari**!
The most delicious, most exclusive, most expensive seafood on the market!

Rex is SO NOT cool!
He can't do that!
He can and he will ... unless WE find the Kraken first.

The race begins!
Charli's crew sets a Kraken pace.
Eat our bubbles, Vancouver!

Rex looked really grumpy.
How could anyone be grumpy with a view like this?
There's so much to see.

There's a school of yellow tang ...
... and a green sea turtle ...
... and a reef manta ray!
Ooh, and look— a giant Pacific octopus!
Think you can beat me, huh?
Prepare to get #WreckedByRex!
Uh-oh.

Bye, wimps!
Eep! Watch out, octopus!
BUMP!

SPLOOT

That prank just got a million views on MeTube.
You're famous, wimps! Hahaha!!

I always wanted to be a MeTube star, but not like this.
As soon as this mess clears, Rex is gonna be sardines on toast.
You've got your head in the clouds. Actually we all have our heads in a cloud.

When the ink finally clears, our crew head for the edge of the reef.
There's Rex up ahead, just past the great white shark.
Shark? Our boat isn't that big ... what if he bites through?

Relax, Rav. A shark can't bite through the walls of the SUB.
That's right, isn't it, Charli?
It wouldn't be interested in us, anyway.
Whoa, what is that?
TIKA TIKA TIKA TIKA
It's a drone.
It came out of Rex's sub. It's carrying chum.
Chum? Whose chum?
It means shark bait.
What is Rex up to?

TIKA TIKA TIKA TIKA TIKA TIKA TIKA TIKA...
SQUELCH
I don't know, but he's not getting his drone back.
Extending mechanical arms!

SPROING!

Almost ...
... gotcha!
TIKA TIKA TIKA TIKA
CLAP!
Meanwhile ...
sniff
sniff

NOM NOM NOM NOM NOM NOM NOM

Uh-oh. Our communications are cut!
The shark bit the SUB!
I told you we needed a bigger boat! Whaddawedo?

Don't panic, Rav. Sal and I prepared for this.
There's only one animal that sharks are afraid of ...
Activating holographic projector.
... the killer whale!
!
Boo.
That shark made a dish of our communications.
Luckily we have a satellite phone for emergencies ...
... but it doesn't work underwater.

The ocean really needs wifi.
So Rex is well ahead. He might find the Kraken before us.
What if we let him?
What? Why?
I've got an idea. Do you think you could hack into Rex's drone?
Meanwhile ...
Hey, fancouvers!
We're approaching the Mariana Trench. Keep your eyes peeled for the Kraken.

Wait ... there it is.
It's hideous. I love it!
After it, crew!
Rex's drone (hacked by Sally)

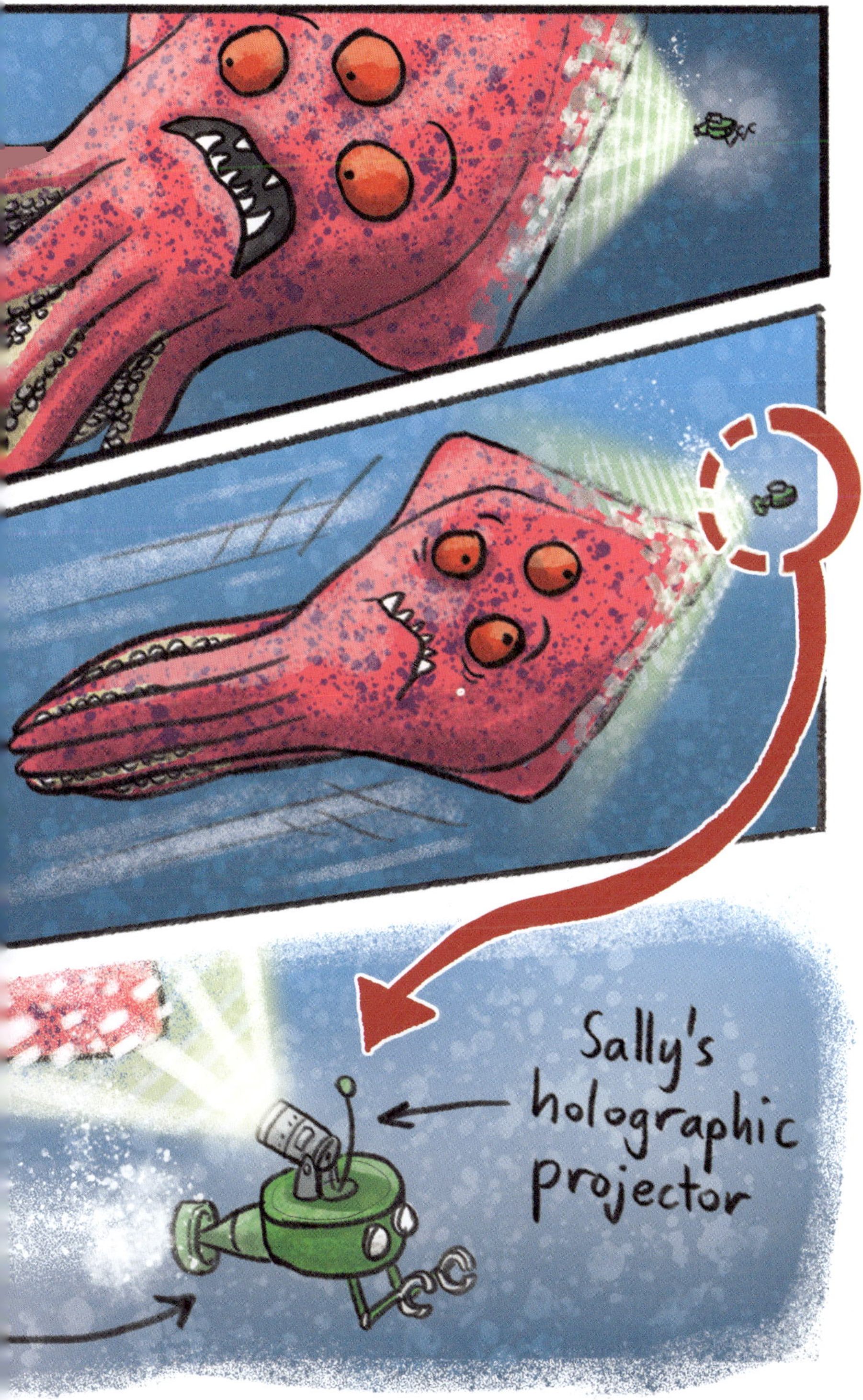
Sally's holographic projector

It worked. We pranked Rex!
Brilliant idea, Charli.
It was a team effort.
What in Neptune's beard ... is that what I think it is?
I-i-it's the ... th-th-the ... th-the ...

... K-Kraken!

We've found it! Huzzah!
Not quite ...

... it's just a giant squid.
'Just'?
Sorry to burst your bubble.

I think I've burst my brain.
Hi, Squiddy!
Wow.
Maybe that fishing crew didn't see 'the Kraken' after all.
Yeah ... maybe they saw Squiddy here and thought she was the Kraken.

Guess who's back, wimps?
!
I see you found the Kraken without me!
KA-POW!
NO!

And that's a wrap.
Rex, let her go!
She's not the Kraken!
Who cares? We'll edit the footage to make it look big and scary.
My **gullible fans** won't know the difference!

Let her go NOW!
Make me.
Sally, may I borrow those gloves?
Be my guest.
No more Miss nice Charli.

You should be nervous, Rex!
NO!
GRAB!

You can't stop me. I'm gonna chop up this squid and sell it for squillions!
Give up already.
Never! Let her go, Rex!
Grrrr. Won't take the hint, huh?
Can you take a HIT?
KONK
WOOP WOOP
That's it!
No one threatens my friends.

Kapow!
KAPOW!
SEVERE DAMAGE SUSTAINED.
AUTOMATIC EMERGENCY EJECT ACTIVATED.
No, no, no ...

NOOOOOOOOOOO!
KSSSHHHH!

You got wrecked! Bye, Rex.
Bad news, crew. Rex damaged our depth control tanks.
We can't surface the SUB.
And that shark cut off our comms, so we can't call for help.
So we're stuck down here?
And sinking fast.
AIEEEE!

We've gotta release Squiddy, before we sink any deeper.
Just because we're trapped, doesn't mean she has to be.
Seeya, Squiddy!

What's the plan, Sally?
I'm thinking.
Please think harder!
I'm trying! If I could get outside the SUB, I could repair the depth control tanks ...
... but the scuba suits aren't rated for this depth. The water pressure would squish me instantly.
What about the satellite phone?
It doesn't work underwater, remember?

Could we build another communications dish?
That's possible ...
Thank goodness.
... I give it a 3% chance of success, but it's possible.
We're all gonna dieeeeeee!
Hey Joe, you look so worried. It's gonna be okay. We'll figure a way out.

What is it, bud? What's ...
Oh.
We've got company.

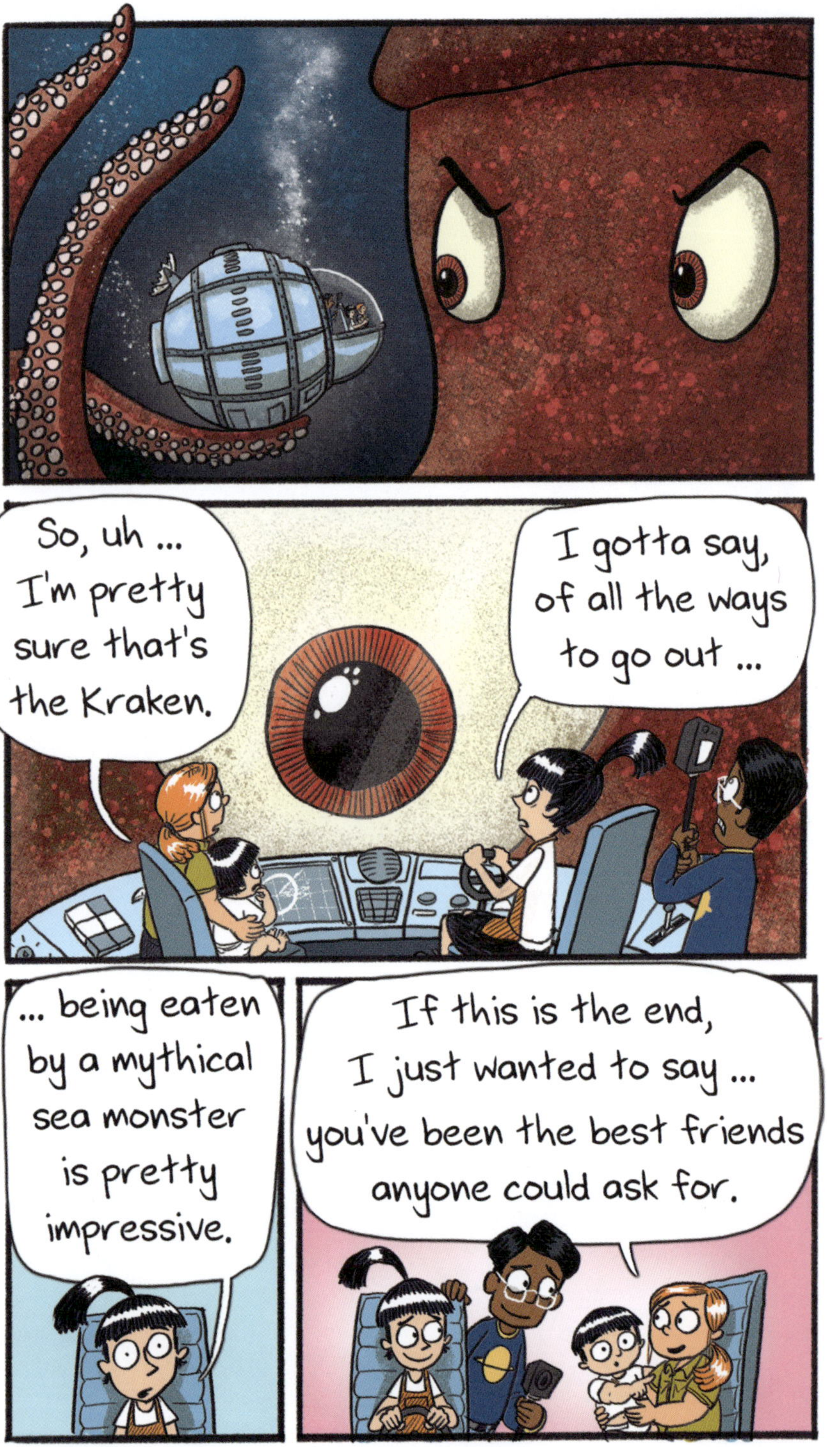

So, uh ... I'm pretty sure that's the Kraken.
I gotta say, of all the ways to go out ...
... being eaten by a mythical sea monster is pretty impressive.
If this is the end, I just wanted to say ... you've been the best friends anyone could ask for.

Hey, look, it's Squiddy!
What are they doing, Charli?
Are they both going to eat us?
No ...
... I think they're communicating.

Well, I hope Squiddy is saying something nice, our lives are in her hands.
Uh, tentacles.
Squiddy's waving bye-bye.
Is that a good thing?
CREEEEAK!
GROAN!
What's happening, Charli?
I'm not sure!
AIEEEE!
ARGHH!
EEEP!

We're done for!
No, Rav. The Kraken is saving us!

Prepare to breach!

KA-SPLOOSH!
PLONK

And so ...
Thank you, Kraken! Thank you, Squiddy!
Dry land, I could kiss you! Mwah!

I've got satellite reception! I'll get Nan to pick us up.
Pah! Bleh!

If we've got reception, we can upload the Kraken footage.
We're going to be famous on MeTube!
About that ... I don't think we should release the Kraken footage. Let's keep it a secret.
Otherwise more awful people like Rex will try to catch it.
Charli's right.
Agreed.
There is ONE bit of video that we should DEFINITELY release, though ...

Thus ends another epic S.Tinker Inc. adventure!

THE END

If you liked these stories,
you're going to want more!
Check out my other awesome
adventures - *Chickensaurus*, *Brobot*
and *Dungzilla*!

JAMES FOLEY
IN ALL NEW FABULOUS COLOUR
DUNGZILLA

JAMES FOLEY
IN ALL NEW FABULOUS COLOUR
CHICKEN-SAURUS

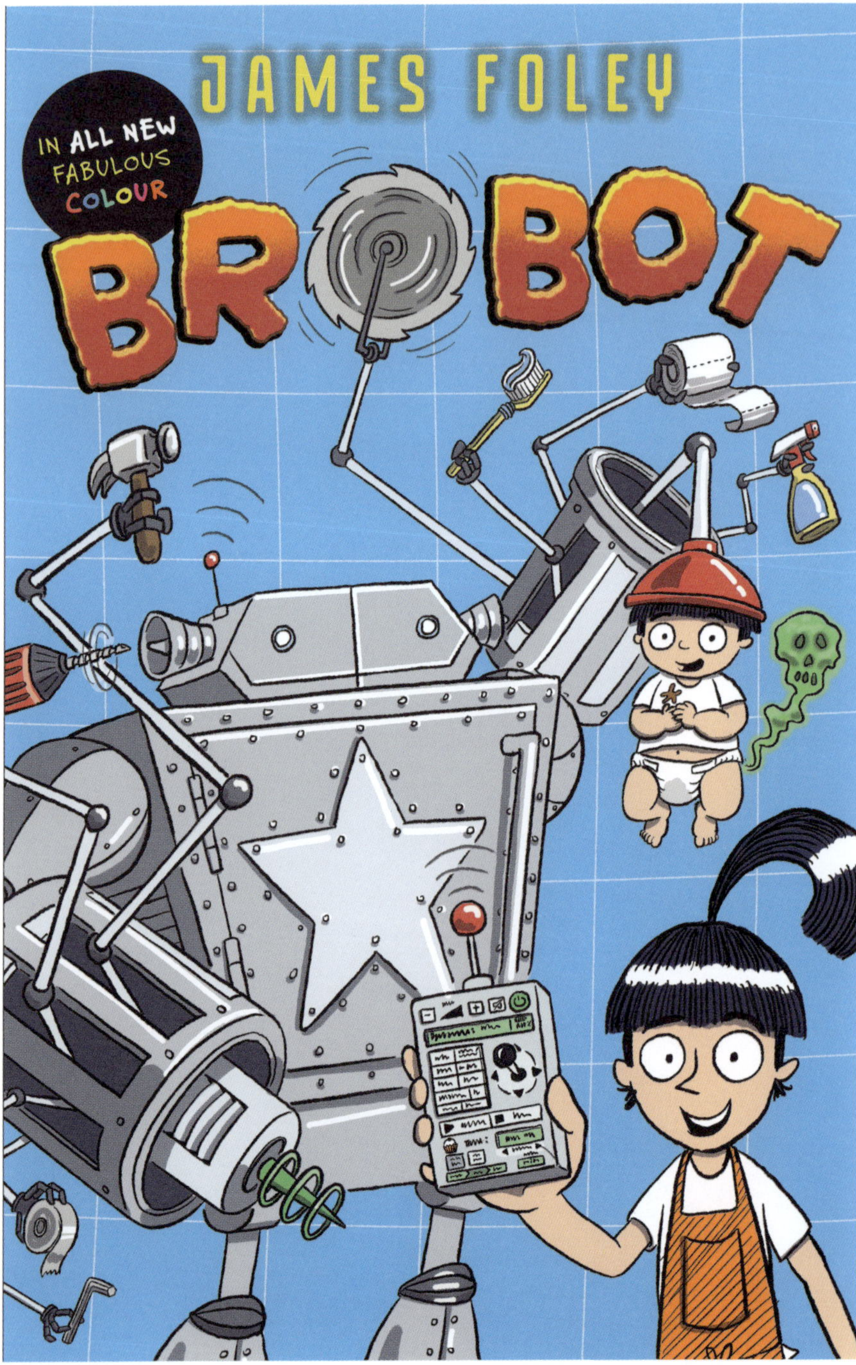
JAMES FOLEY
IN ALL NEW FABULOUS COLOUR
BROBOT

JAMES FOLEY

James Foley makes children's books for children who read books. If you're a child and you're eating his books, you're doing it wrong. You might know his picture book *Stellarphant* or his graphic novel series *Secret Agent Mole*. He lives in Perth with his wife, Renae, their two kids and a labrador called Frankie. He's an ambassador for Books In Homes and Room To Read; a massive Marvel movie nerd; and comes from a long line of queuing enthusiasts. Legend says James can grow a beard in an afternoon.

jamesfoley.com.au

This edition first published 2024 by
FREMANTLE PRESS
Fremantle Press Inc. trading as Fremantle Press
PO Box 158, North Fremantle, Western Australia, 6159
fremantlepress.com.au

Gastronauts was first published by Fremantle Press in 2018.
The original version of 'Get Kraken' first appeared in *The School Magazine*, 2021.

Designed by James Foley and Rebecca Mills.
Gastronauts colourisation by Paulina Gamez.
Printed by Leo Paper Products Ltd. Guangdong, China.

NATIONAL LIBRARY OF AUSTRALIA
A catalogue record for this book is available from the National Library of Australia

ISBN 9781760993122 (paperback)
ISBN 9781760993771 (ebook)

GOVERNMENT OF WESTERN AUSTRALIA
Department of Local Government, Sport and Cultural Industries
lotterywest

Fremantle Press is supported by the State Government through the Department of Local Government, Sport and Cultural Industries.

Fremantle Press respectfully acknowledges the Whadjuk people of the Noongar nation as the Traditional Owners and Custodians of the land where we work in Walyalup.

FSC www.fsc.org
MIX
Paper | Supporting responsible forestry
FSC® C020056